The Adventures of Princess Jah yeh ee

By: Devin Arlean Patterson

Illustrated by: Devin Arlean Patterson

There once was a beautiful princess named princess Jah yeh ee who was the princess of Tan Zambia Africa.

Princess jah yeh ee was extremely shy and reserved, she loved helping others and spreading love everywhere she went. That is her superpower, she is the giver of love.

One day she walked out of the kingdom and noticed loud shouting. She ran over to where the shouting was heard and noticed a girl picking on another.

The girl was calling the other names such as ugly and chubby. Princess jah yeh ee immediately stopped the girl by saying "why are you picking on this beautiful queen?"

The girl replies by saying "look at her she's ugly and fat." Princess jah yeh ee tells the girl "you must be mistaken? I see a beautiful brown queen in my presence, and that goes for you as well and you should treat each other as such.

The girl looks at the other, then princess jah yeh ee   and immediately apologizes to the young girl for her harsh words. The young girl then accepts her apology and they hug and become friends.

An Just like that princess jah yeh ee saves the day with her powerful words.

The end.

www.ingramcontent.com/pod-product-compliance
Lightning Source LLC
Chambersburg PA
CBHW042112040426
42448CB00002B/236